Agent Extreme

By Louise Park
Illustrated by Ben Wood

Pearson Australia
(a division of Pearson Australia Group Pty Ltd)
707 Collins Street, Melbourne, Victoria 3008
PO Box 23360, Melbourne, Victoria 8012
www.pearson.com.au

First published 2014 by Pearson Australia
2018 2017 2016
10 9 8 7 6 5 4 3 2

Publisher: Sabine Bolick
Project Managers: Tamara Pirois and Rachel Davis
Lead Editors: Kerry Nagle and Beth Zeme
Editors: Philip Bryan and Beth Zeme
Cover and Series Designers: Jenny Grigg and Anne Donald
Designers: Nina Heryanto and Leigh Ashforth
Copyright & Pictures Editor: Julia Weaver
Mac Operator: Rob Curulli
Cover art: Ben Wood
Illustrator: Ben Wood

Printed in Australia by the SOS Print + Media Group

ISBN 978 1 4860 0756 1

Pearson Australia Group Pty Ltd ABN 40 004 245 943

Acknowledgements
Every effort has been made to trace and acknowledge copyright. However, if any infringement has occurred, the publishers tender their apologies and invite the copyright holders to contact them.

Disclaimer
Some of the images used in *Agent Extreme* might have associations with deceased Indigenous Australians. Please be aware that these images might cause sadness or distress in Aboriginal or Torres Strait Islander communities.

Contents

Chapter 1

Do you have what it takes?

Max Werriby dropped his swimming bag at the front door and raced his brother into the kitchen. "Beat you!" he shouted, as he grabbed the cereal box from the pantry. He took two bowls from the cupboard. "Mum is at footy trials with Ed."

"Oh, he'll make the A team for sure," Tom said, joining his brother at the kitchen bench. "He's a star, like me. So, what happened to you Maxy-boy? Too water logged and science-mad to play ball?"

Max shrugged. "You need new material, Tom," he said, trying to sound casual. "Ribbing me about that doesn't get to me anymore."

But the truth was that it *did* get to Max. In fact, it drove him crazy. Max was 12 years old and he was sandwiched between two brothers who were serious soccer legends and all-round sports stars.

Somehow, Max had missed out on the ball skills in the family.

The front door opened and Tom shouted to his younger brother. "Hey, Ed, Did you make it into the A's?"

"Yep," Ed said with a grin, as he walked down the hall.

"Go *you*!" Max said. "That's great."

"It's fabulous," Mum said. "We're going to celebrate tonight at Lucky's Pizza. Have you put your wet swimming gear in the laundry, Max?" Then she headed upstairs.

Max stetched his arm along the bench and rested his head on it. He watched as Tom took the stairs two at a time with his long legs. He's so tall, thought Max, not like me. If only I could be a star at something!

And that's when Max noticed what was on the back of the cereal box.

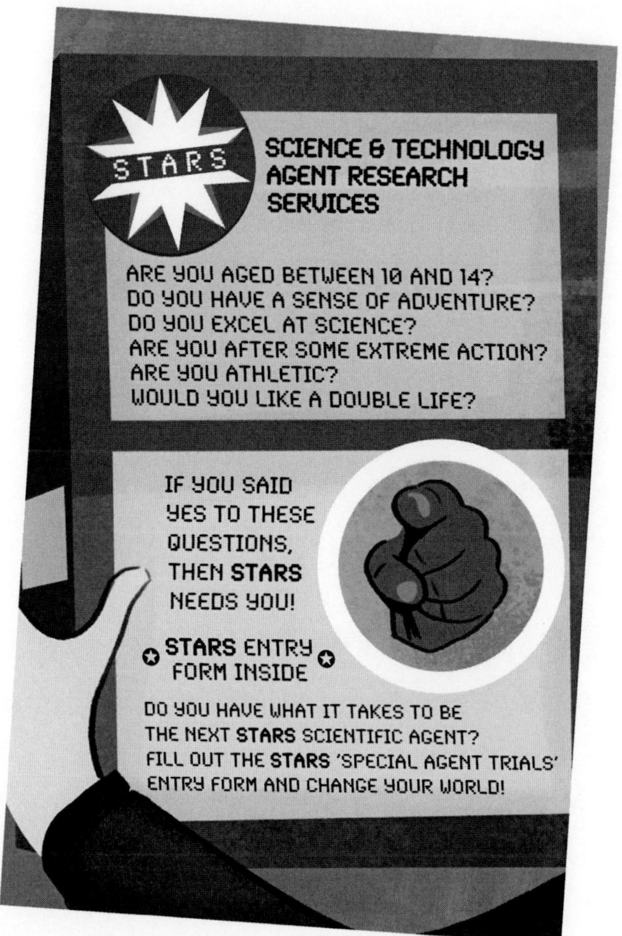

"I'd love to have a double life!" Max said to himself, as he read the rest of the ad. "How cool would that be!" Then he laughed and shook his head. "You're such a loser, Max Werriby. I mean, an ad on the back of a cereal box? Get real!"

Max pulled out his wet training gear from his bag. He hung his goggles on the hook in the laundry and threw his wet gear into the laundry tub. On his way back through the kitchen he grabbed the cereal box and tucked it tightly under his arm. *Still, there's no harm in sending in an application,* he thought. *It's not like I'd get picked, even if it was real.*

Then he raced up the stairs and hid the cereal box at the back of his wardrobe.

*

As soon as the car was in the garage, Max was out and at the door that led into the house.

"Thanks for taking us to Lucky's," said Max. "I'm pretty tired from swimming training. I think I'll just go up to bed."

"Okay," said Mum, giving him a hug.

Max picked up their new puppy, Winnie-the-poodle, and headed straight for his room. He took the cereal box from his wardrobe and sat down at his desk. "Science and Technology Agent Research Services," Max read aloud. "I win medals for science, Winnie! I wonder what I'd be doing if I got picked? Maybe I'd get to conduct experiments in a super-cool lab."

Max rummaged through the cereal and found the sealed package containing the forms.

There's some pretty weird questions here, thought Max as he filled out the form. Why do they need to know if I panic under pressure?

Max popped the form in the pocket of his school blazer. "I'll post it on the way to school tomorrow. Wish me luck, Winnie-the-poodle." And he put the pup in her basket and got ready for bed.

Chapter 2

The next level

Two weeks later, on a Saturday morning at 9:30 a.m., Max Werriby was standing outside the local public library. This can't be right, he thought, looking at the address STARS had given him. I knew it! It's a scam. I should've realised when I got the competition acceptance letter.

"Um ... hi," said a voice, breaking into his thoughts. "You're holding the same card I am. So, any minute now someone is going to jump out from behind a bush with a camera and say *'Gotcha!'* right?"

Max turned to see who owned the voice. It was a girl about his age. She had shiny black hair pulled back in a ponytail and wore cargo pants and a sweatshirt that said 'Science Rocks!'.

"Yeah, I reckon," said Max. "It's some kind of joke, for sure."

"It sounded so awesome," the girl replied, slapping the card against her thigh. "I'm Lillie. Lillie-Lee actually, but I prefer just Lillie."

"Hi, I'm Max. It did sound too good to be true," said Max. "I guess we may as well go."

"Hang on," Lillie said. "Maybe STARS has moved and someone in the library will know their new address, or something."

Max shrugged. "Let's try," he said.

Lillie and Max made their way to the front desk. "Hi," said Max, holding up his STARS card. "We're looking for this place and wondered if you could help us."

"Lillie-Lee Evans and Maximillion Werriby," the librarian said, smiling at them both. "We've been expecting you."

A
B

Max and Lillie exchanged a quick look. But before either of them could speak, the attendant said "Here are your instructions. Good luck," and he handed each of them an envelope. Then he picked up a stack of books and headed for the shelves.

Lillie looked at Max. "*Maximillion?*" she said with a giggle. "That's worse than *Lillie-Lee-tiny-little-bee*! That's what my older sister calls me. I'm the short one in the family."

Max grinned. "Both my brothers are really tall," he confided. He could tell he was going to be friends with this girl.

Max opened his envelope and read the instructions: **"Insert this card into the slot in the lift. Select level 1."** Max looked at Lillie. "But the library doesn't have a Level 1."

"Mine says the same," Lillie said. "Weird. Come on, let's do it! What have we got to lose?"

Max led the way to the lift at the back of the library. "Great," he said as he looked at the panel. "We're headed for the car park."

"Just push the button," urged Lillie.

The lift doors opened and they both stepped in. Max inserted his card into the slot below the control panel and the doors closed.

"*Woah!*" said Max, taking a step back. "Look at the panel. It's growing buttons!"

"*Max!*" cried Lillie. "The competition is real!" and she leant across and pushed the button for Level 1.

The lift began to move, and it went up rather than down. Then a voice came through the lift speaker: "Level 1: Science and Technology Agent Research Services".

"*Yes!*" shouted Max, as the lift came to a stop. "It is real, but where this level is beats me."

The lift doors opened and Max and Lillie stood staring out. "Am I dreaming?" Lillie asked with wide eyes. "It's like something from a sci-fi movie."

There were huge glass computer screens taking up one long wall with people standing and working at them. The benches were covered with gadgets and hand-held computers. Five tube portals stood on the other side of the room.

Max and Ellie were ushered into the high-tech lab by a woman in a white lab coat. Her name tag said Agent Mendez.

"Hurry up, you two," she said as she herded them towards three boys standing over by a workstation. "Congratulations on making it into the STARS test mission. Five were chosen but there will only be one winner."

"*T-t-test mission*," stammered Max. "I thought we'd be working in a lab."

"Good heavens, no!" said Agent Mendez. "You applied and have been selected to complete a trial mission in the hope that you will become a STARS agent. STARS is a scientific agency that combats scientific and environmental evil. The successful candidate from this test mission will go through our special–agent training program and eventually become a STARS top-secret field agent."

Science Rocks!

Suddenly everything fell into place for Max. I could become a secret scientific agent, he thought, excited.

"Where are these two levels, exactly?" Lillie asked. "You can't see them from the outside."

"Here at STARS we have an app for everything," answered Agent Mendez. "We like our location to remain secret, so we simply hide our headquarters using one of our apps. Now, we'll be sending you into three very harsh environments and you'll have to use your own scientific knowledge of how best to survive each one to complete the set task."

Max looked at the computer screens. **"Extreme deep, extreme dry and extreme cold,"** he read aloud. **"The animals and plants that can survive there have adapted over years to be able to live there."**

Max turned to Agent Mendez. "We don't have years to adapt," he asked. "How are we supposed to manage?"

"Our agents are always equipped with the latest technology and gadgetry, as will you be," Mendez answered. "For this little mission, you'll be teleported into virtual environments that we've created, and we'll monitor your performance all the way.

"Positioned in each environment is a pure silicon crystal quartz rod," said Mendez. "These rods are your targets. Your task is to be the first to reach them and touch them. You will all be given the same mission gear and gadgets. You will each face the same obstacles.

"When you land in an environment, you will all be at the exact same distance from the target – although you will not be together. You will be given equal opportunity to win, but only one of you will make it through and become a STARS agent."

And it's going to be me that makes it through, thought Max, with sudden determination.

Chapter 3

Adapt and morph

Max and Lillie stood with the three other successful candidates in the STARS mission prep room. "I'm the youngest here," Lillie whispered to Max. "You and Jack are 12, Sam is 13, and AJ is 14. I'm the only girl."

"You love science," Max whispered. "It says so on your top. You'll be fine."

"Listen carefully," Mendez said to the group. "Once a rod has been touched by one of you, the race in that environment is over. Your time and position at the time the rod is touched will be recorded."

Mendez looked at them, one by one. "Then you will all be automatically teleported to the next environment, regardless of where you are in the race."

"Then we race for the next rod in the next environment," said Sam.

Max stole a quick look at his opponent. Sam was quite a lot taller than he was.

"Correct," Agent Mendez said. "Three environments, three rods, one winner." Then she went over to the back cabinet to retrieve some gadgets.

"This'll be easy," AJ said, under his breath. "I'm up against three babies and a girl."

Lillie glared at AJ. Max gave her a reassuring nudge.

"Ladies first," Agent Mendez said, as she returned to the group and handed Lillie a watch. "Some of our best agents are females, Lillie-Lee."

"Wow," Lillie replied, as she strapped on the watch. "It's more like a small computer."

"Correct," Agent Mendez said, as she handed the others their watches. "It has a navigation system in it to help you reach your targets. The stopwatch will tell you how much time you have and your position in the race. The watch is also loaded with a large database of apps. You can search for apps by scrolling down the list or by entering what you want into the search bar. The apps allow you to adapt and cope in the environments – provided you choose wisely. The apps and your clever thinking will be critical to your success.

"Most importantly, once you use an app and change your appearance, you will not be able to see your watches anymore. Don't be alarmed by this. Your watch will be internalised into your new shape. All you need to do is think about what you want or need and it will happen. For example, if you want to know how much time you have left, simply think *stopwatch*, and a screen showing the stopwatch will appear in front of you."

"Can we use as many apps as we want in each environment?" Max asked.

"Only two apps in each environment, I'm afraid," answered Mendez. "Fifteen minutes has been provided for each environment. If the target isn't reached by any of you in that time, you'll all be teleported to the next environment and another 15-minute counter will begin on your screens. If anyone makes poor choices and gets into trouble, we'll know and bring them straight back here.

"Now, let's get you all dressed and on your way. In the change rooms, you'll each find our specifically-designed and very top-secret adapta-morph suits. All-in-ones, I'm afraid, but they are extraordinary and irreplaceable in the field. You won't need shoes or anything else. Be on the portal pads in five minutes."

The five recruits entered their change rooms. After a few minutes, Max knocked gently on Lillie's door. "I look like some biohazard weirdo in this suit," he whispered.

Max raised his arms. "My suit has hands and feet in it. This is a serious all-in-one."

Lillie stepped out of her change room and laughed. "It's not how I thought a secret agent would look! And don't forget the hood and face screen."

Mendez clapped her hands. "Hurry along," she said. "The others are ready and waiting."

"I'm about to be teleported," Max said, stepping onto his podium. "Cool. Good luck, guys. See you underwater."

Everyone responded with well wishes, except for AJ, who sneered.

"Teleporting in 10 seconds," said Mendez, heading for the control panels. "May the best agent win. The underwater environment is first. Take a big deep breath now and hold it."

Max took a huge breath and held it. Then the portal tubes filled with light. Max looked down at his body and watched as it disappeared before his eyes.

Chapter 4

Extreme deep

Max crashed down hard onto the sea floor. I'm glad swimming training has helped me hold my breath for a long time, he thought. He held his arm out in front of him and used the light on his watch to illuminate the dark water.

Max was surrounded by branchy tree-type coral, fan-shaped coral, fine-hairy coral – and even coral that looked like human brains. There was every colour he could imagine, from deep pinks and purples to reds, yellows and oranges.

The coral harboured an abundance of marine life, with different kinds of fish, crabs and other sea creatures swimming in and around them.

I'm in a deep sea coral haven, Max thought. Coral that doesn't need sunlight to survive. But where are the others?

Max was getting desperate to let out his breath and breathe again. He quickly scrolled through the apps on his watch and stopped at a GILLS subset.

Gills would be very handy right now, he thought. Then a message flashed on his screen:

LOW FREQUENCY PULSING ACTIVATED

Oh, no! thought Max. Sharks have adapted to pick up sound vibrations from miles away. That's how they find their prey – and it's going to be me! He frantically typed in

STONEFISH

just as a school of sharks arrived directly above him. He found the stonefish app and selected it.

Instantly, Max found that he could breathe easy again. Simultaneously, he felt his body shrink and change. Before he knew it, Max was only about 40 centimetres long and resting quietly on the sea floor like a hard grey stone. He was perfectly camouflaged. *These apps are awesome,* he thought. *I bet I have the needle-like dorsal-fin spines that will poison anything that touches them, too. But I do feel like a weird bowl of jelly.*

Max stayed perfectly still and watched as the school of sharks swam around looking for their prey before moving off. He waited until the last shark had left and then thought about the time he'd lost. Suddenly a clear screen appeared and floated in front of him. It showed 02·38 and counting.

I might have saved myself by using camouflage, Max thought, *but now I'm stuck here like a rock! I don't even know the location of the crystal rod or where I am in relation to it.*

The screen floating before Max updated and showed a chart that looked a bit like a radar map. Max could see how far away the crystal rod was and his position on the map. Great! I'm, like, 10 kilometres away, he thought. And the others are way ahead of me in the race now. But why isn't Sam on the screen?

I can't worry about Sam, thought Max. I need to get moving fast. Think *speed.* Max concentrated on thinking *sailfish*, knowing it was the fastest fish in the sea. The screen flashed with the words:

SAILFISH TAKEN: LILLIE-LEE

Max smiled. "Good on her," he said to himself, and he turned his thoughts to *striped marlin*, hoping his guess was right.

The screen flashed with the words:

STRIPED MARLIN TAKEN: AJ

Guess that makes sense, since it's the second-fastest fish and he's coming second.

Max remembered the sharks above him. Blue sharks can swim really fast.

1ST: LILLIE-LEE
WINNING TIME: 09·13
APPS USED: PEACOCK FLOUNDER FOR GILLS & CAMOUFLAGE, & SAILFISH FOR SPEED
DISTANCE COVERED: 15 KM

2ND: AJ
APPS USED: STRIPED MARLIN & BLUEFIN TUNA FOR GILLS & SPEED
DISTANCE COVERED: 14.9 KM

3RD: MAX
APPS USED: STONFISH FOR GILLS & CAMOUFLAGE, & BLUE SHARK FOR SPEED
DISTANCE COVERED: 13.8 KM

4TH: JACK
APPS USED: OCTOPUS FOR GILLS & CAMOUFLAGE, & SWORDFISH FOR SPEED
DISTANCE COVERED: 13.2 KM

REMOVED FROM RACE: SAM
REASON: FROZE UNDER PRESSURE.
TIME BROUGHT BACK TO STARS LAB: 00·50
DISTANCE COVERED: 0.0 KM

Blue shark! he thought.

Immediately, Max felt his body morphing again. Now Max was long and sleek, with large pectoral fins. Max repeated the words *navigational guidance* over and over in his head until his route appeared on the floating screen in front of him. *"Go! Go! Go!"* he said to himself, as he and the screen cut through the water at a speed of 70 kilometres per hour.

As Max got closer to his target, he could see a large sailfish and a striped marlin racing towards the glowing crystal rod. He watched as the sailfish charged ahead to touch the crystal rod first. Then Max's screen updated with a score chart. He had just enough time to read it before he was gone.

Chapter 5

Extreme dry

Max fell face first onto hot, dry red sand. Sweat was already running down his face and back. He didn't waste a second. Max knew he'd been teleported to a hot, dusty, sandy desert. He also knew that he needed to be able to cope with the harsh conditions, retain water and food, and be able to move as fast as he could in the extreme heat.

Max keyed CAMEL into his watch's search engine as fast as he could. "I got it first!" he shouted out loud as the app popped up. He clicked on the app and the morphing began.

I'm loving this! Max thought. I'm a single-humped dromedary and I'm so tall! I've got fat in my hump, and water in the lining of my stomach. I don't feel thirsty or hungry at all. And best of all, my wool coat keeps out the heat of the day and the cold of the night.

Max concentrated on the route and the screen appeared. Only five kilometres to the target and no one's started yet, he thought, looking at the screen floating just in front of him. I could win this leg of the race.

Max started trotting in the direction of the crystal rod. He could see on the screen that he was keeping ahead of everyone else. Endless-looking flat landscape with scorching sand and harsh sunlight lay ahead of him. With each trot, Max could feel his wide, padded feet grip the sand and prevent him from sinking into it. Max knew the camel could gallop faster than it was going, but he wanted to conserve energy until he really needed it.

When Max was at the 3-kilometre point, he stopped and looked around, curious to see what form the others had chosen.

Not too far away on his left, Max could see something with a tiny body and big ears moving fairly quickly. The fox blended in so well with the environment that he almost missed it. Lillie's so smart, he thought. She's picked something that has the added protection of camouflage.

A little further over from Lillie, Max saw a fat sand rat that made him laugh as well as a camel could. What a weird sound, thought Max. But seeing AJ as a rat was just too funny.

Next, Max turned to the right to look for Jack. Way off in the distance he could just make out the horns of an antelope. They never need to drink, they get water from their food, he thought, but they're too slow. Time for me to move a bit faster too, I reckon.

Max took off at a gallop and was making good, swift progress. And then, in the blink of an eye, a strong wind blew fast and hard across the desert. It brought with it clouds of sand and dust so dense that it blocked out the sun.

I can barely see the screen in front of me, Max thought, as he squinted through his two rows of long eyelashes. At least these eyelashes keep out a lot of the sand and dust. And my nostrils have closed. Camels are so cool! I won't even need to morph again with a bit of luck. And then he noticed that Jack wasn't appearing on the screen. Only three left now. Then he galloped on as fast as possible through the blinding sandstorm.

With only 300 metres to go, Max still couldn't see the crystal rod and his screen was getting harder and harder to see.

Just then, the noise of wings flapping broke Max's thoughts and he looked up as a large shadow moved over him.

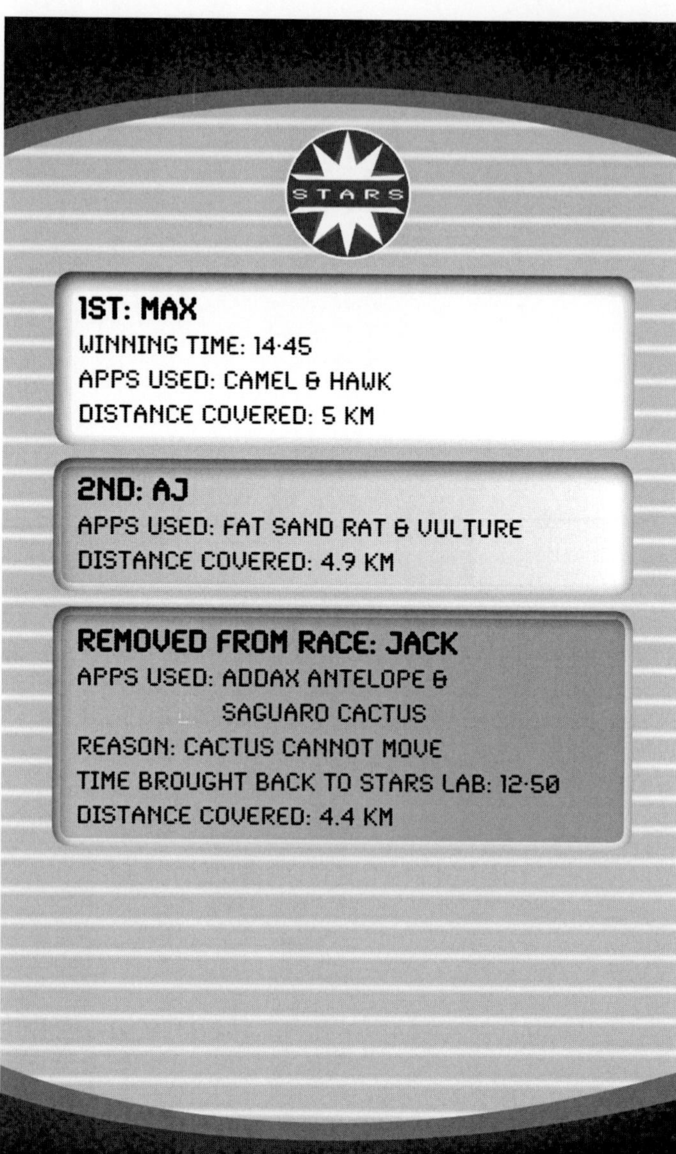
STARS
1ST: MAX
WINNING TIME: 14·45
APPS USED: CAMEL & HAWK
DISTANCE COVERED: 5 KM
2ND: AJ
APPS USED: FAT SAND RAT & VULTURE
DISTANCE COVERED: 4.9 KM
REMOVED FROM RACE: JACK
APPS USED: ADDAX ANTELOPE & SAGUARO CACTUS
REASON: CACTUS CANNOT MOVE
TIME BROUGHT BACK TO STARS LAB: 12·50
DISTANCE COVERED: 4.4 KM

Oh, no! Max thought, as a vulture with a pale pink head and massive dark wings swooped down over him and towards the target.

He then spied a strange-looking bird alongside of him. I'm going to lose again! *Hawk!* Quick! *I want to be a hawk!* As he morphed, he took one last look at the screen. Then he headed straight for his target, eyes closed against sand and dust.

Max reached the crystal first and tapped it with his beak. Instantly the sandstorm vanished and the scorecard flashed onto his screen.

Chapter 6

Extreme cold

Max now found himself standing with Lillie and AJ on an ice floe that was floating on the surface of the freezing Arctic Sea.

AJ was the first to speak. "This is different," he said, tapping his watch. "My watch isn't working. Why are we stranded here together?"

Max and Lillie both looked at their watches. "Maybe it's too cold here for them to work," Lillie said, her teeth chattering.

"Don't be dumb," AJ sniped. "As if they'd make watches that can't work in their own virtual environments."

"Well, something strange is going on," said Max, looking around. "I say we work out a way to get to land. This floe isn't that big. It could break apart at any minute and we aren't dressed to survive the freezing water temperature."

"The wind is picking up," said Lillie. "It's making it colder. We need to conserve heat. We should get down low and huddle together."

"She's right," said Max. "At least it's blowing us towards shore." He crouched down and huddled with Lillie. AJ remained standing. He was shaking badly.

The wind suddenly became a gust and the floe began to glide quickly towards the shore. "Nearly there," Max said. "But when we're ashore we're going to have to get out of this wind."

The floe crashed against the snow-covered shore and Max and Lillie jumped off. AJ followed, but he was moving very stiffly.

"Look, it's a big screen," Lillie said pointing in front of them. "We have to morph to climb this mountain. Then there are toboggans at the top that we must use to ride down the other side to the crystal rod – without our navigation systems!"

AJ looked at the screen, and then at his watch, and realised that it was now working. He tried to key in letters or scroll for an app but his fingers seemed to be frozen. He watched as Lillie morphed into an arctic wolf and began running up the hill. He continued tapping frantically while Max morphed into a polar bear and bounded up the mountain after Lillie.

Finally, AJ got his fingers to work and chose ARCTIC FOX. He morphed straight away and sprinted off after Lillie and Max. He had some ground to make up.

Bear, wolf and fox scrambled and climbed up the snowy slope while fierce winds blew down, picking up snow and ice as they went.

This blizzard is slowing me down, thought Max. I can't even see where Lillie and AJ are, let alone the top of the mountain.

Max's feet were padded and covered in fur but they were starting to ache. I must have climbed three or four kilometres by now, he thought.

Finally, the ground began to level out and Max found himself standing on a small flat area. No blinding snowstorm up here, he thought, as he looked around. But that's one massive ski run in front of me, with a lot of frozen trees. Should be awesome on a toboggan!

Then Max looked at his body. Oh yeah, just one small problem, he thought. I'm big, fat and furry! Don't know how handy that's going to be on a toboggan.

Max padded over to where two toboggans stood upright in the snow. One was long and the other short. Someone's already made it to here, he thought. I wonder how far behind I am?

Max pushed at the longer toboggan with his paw, and as soon as he touched it his body began to morph back to human form.

Max felt the loss of fat beneath his skin first and he started to shiver. As he shrank he lost his luxurious coat of white fur and was back in his bright orange adapta-morph suit. I prefer fur, he thought, jumping on to his toboggan.

As Max took off down the slope, he heard a growl and took a quick look behind him. An arctic fox was standing on the top of the mountain glaring at Max.

Max flew down the slope navigating frozen trees, bumps and jumps easily. He could see Lillie not too far in front of him now. He took the next bend at a cracking pace and then the view opened up before him. It was a steep downhill run with some rocks on either side of it. At the very bottom of the run Max could see the crystal rod with a flag flying above it.

Lillie had begun traversing, finding the slope too steep and Max was gaining on her.

All at once Max heard a loud swooshing noise as AJ overtook him. He's out of control, thought Max, watching as AJ tobogganed vertically towards Lillie. And then, in the blink of an eye, Lillie had been sent tumbling into snow-covered rocks.

"Are you hurt?" asked Max breathlessly, pulling up beside Lillie.

"Not really," she said a little shakily. "But my toboggan's broken. You go. You can still beat AJ!"

"With you," Max said. "Jump on! Hurry."

Lillie climbed on the toboggan and held on to Max's waist, and then they were off.

After the collision, AJ had slowed slightly in an effort to gain more control on the steep slope. Max could see him just ahead and there were only about 100 metres left. He pointed his toboggan straight down and gained on AJ. They were neck and neck to the finishing line … and suddenly all three were gone in flash.

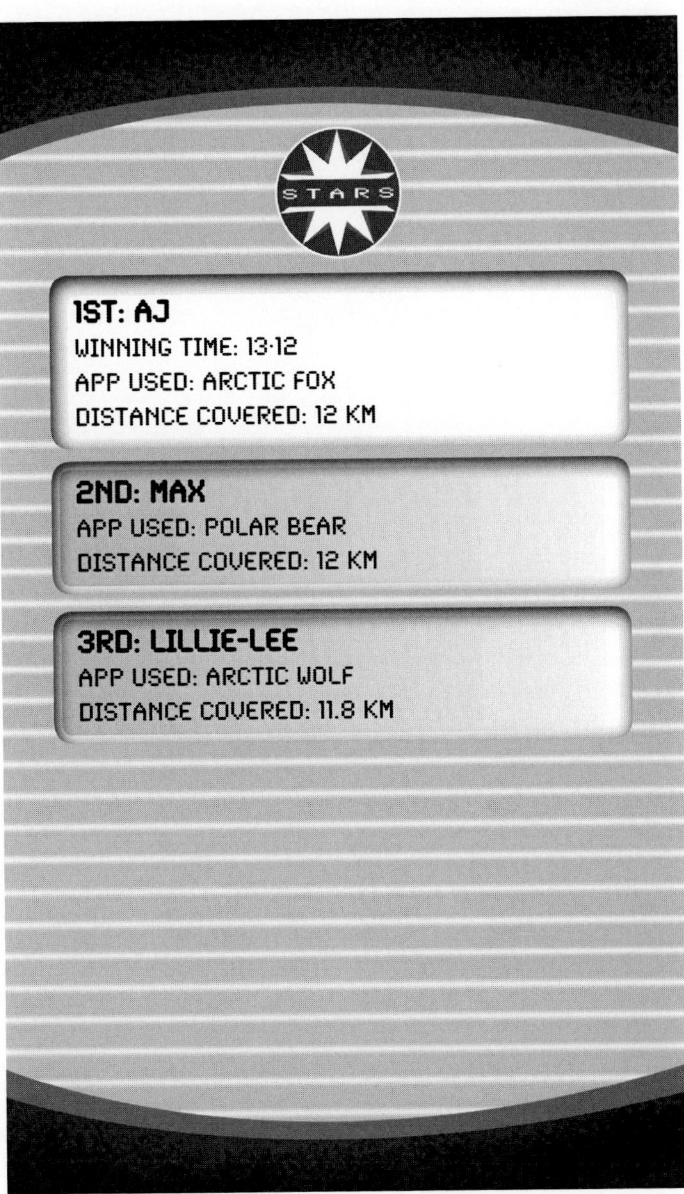
STARS
1ST: AJ
WINNING TIME: 13·12
APP USED: ARCTIC FOX
DISTANCE COVERED: 12 KM
2ND: MAX
APP USED: POLAR BEAR
DISTANCE COVERED: 12 KM
3RD: LILLIE-LEE
APP USED: ARCTIC WOLF
DISTANCE COVERED: 11.8 KM

Chapter 7

Selection time

Max, Lillie and AJ stepped down from their portals to join Agent Mendez, Jack and Sam. Max's heart was still racing from the race.

"That was a most impressive effort from all three of you," Mendez said, with enthusiasm. "You each won a leg of this race and so, to find an overall winner, we must review all of your performances. But first, take off your headgear.

"In the extreme deep," went on Agent Mendez, "Lillie-Lee chose quickly and cleverly. She went for camouflage."

Mendez looked at them. “However, Lillie-Lee also went for something that could keep moving and be safe from prey. AJ showed that he was a risk-taker. He escaped the sharks this time, but it was a big gamble. Max made solid choices. Jack made the best of what apps were left, but overall he had slow reaction times.”

Agent Mendez looked at Sam. “Sam tried hard, but he was dropped in this leg.”

Sam gave a shrug and said, “Looks like the double life isn’t for me.”

“Let’s move on to the second part of the race,” said Agent Mendez, smiling at Sam. “In the extreme heat, Jack’s slow reaction times meant his choices were poor. Although antelopes are well adapted to the desert, the sandstorm proved too much. Jack, you morphed into something that could withstand the storm, but you couldn’t move and that put you out of the race.”

“It wasn’t the smartest choice,” Jack acknowledged. “These guys were way better.”

"Indeed," Mendez said. "By comparison, Max's reaction times were sensational."

"Thanks," said Max. He felt quite proud of himself.

"AJ did what sand rats do best in storms and burrowed. You lost some time there, AJ, but you made it up very well indeed. And Lillie-Lee chose protection and speed and put in a solid effort on this leg.

"Heading into the last leg, we knew we had three very worthwhile contenders for the position. We needed to really see what you were made of, so we mixed it up a little. What we observed was very interesting, indeed.

"Lillie-Lee's ability to think under pressure on that floe was outstanding. AJ's determination to go solo without the help of the others was admirable, but showed that you aren't a team player. If that wipeout hadn't happened, who knows who the winner of the last leg might have been.

"And now for the last two," said Mendez.

"What we *do* know," said Mendez, "is that Max and Lillie-Lee have the makings of the best agent partnership, a partnership that STARS needs.

"It is for this reason that we are awarding two places in the agent training program to Lillie-Lee and Max. Congratulations to both of you."

Lillie squealed and jumped up and down. "I can't believe it! I'm *sooo* happy. Thank you, thank you!"

Max was so shocked that he stood with his mouth open not saying anything for a minute. Then he finally said "We're both in, Lillie! How great is that? We're going to be scientific agents. Go *us*!"